I'M ALLERGIC TO PEANUTS

By Maria Nelson

Gareth Stevens
PUBLISHING

Please visit our website, www.garethstevens.com. For a free color catalog of all our high-quality books, call toll free 1-800-542-2595 or fax 1-877-542-2596.

Library of Congress Cataloging-in-Publication Data

Nelson, Maria.
I'm allergic to peanuts / by Maria Nelson.
  p. cm. — (I'm allergic)
Includes index.
ISBN 978-1-4824-0975-8 (pbk.)
ISBN 978-1-4824-0976-5 (6-pack)
ISBN 978-1-4824-0974-1 (library binding)
1. Food allergy in children — Juvenile literature. 2. Peanuts — Juvenile literature.
 I. Nelson, Maria. II. Title.
RJ386.5 N45 2014
618.92—d23

Published in 2015 by
Gareth Stevens Publishing
111 East 14th Street, Suite 349
New York, NY 10003

Copyright © 2015 Gareth Stevens Publishing

Designer: Nicholas Domiano
Editor: Kristen Rajczak

Photo credits: Cover, p. 1 (girl) Jill Chen/Shutterstock.com; cover, p. 1 (peanut butter, Plate) Stockbyte/Thinkstock.com; pp. 3–24 (background texture), 5, 21 iStock/Thinkstock.com; p. 7 Cavan Images/Stone/Getty Images; p. 9 Stuart Miles/Thinkstock.com; p. 11 Stockbyte/ Thinkstock.com; p. 13 Andy Crawford/Dorling Kindersley/Getty Images; p. 15 overcrew/ Shutterstock.com; p. 17 Peter Dazeley/Photographer's Choice/Getty Images; p. 19 Monkey Business Images/Shutterstock.com.

Printed in the United States of America

CPSIA compliance information: Batch #CS15GS: For further information contact Gareth Stevens, New York, New York at 1-800-542-2595.

CONTENTS

Boldface words appear in the glossary.

Peanut Trouble

A peanut **allergy** is one of the most common food allergies. The body **reacts** to peanut **proteins**. It fights them as it would other harmful matter, like germs.

Allergic reactions to peanuts happen just minutes after someone eats food that has peanuts in it or that peanuts have touched. Breathing in products such as peanut flour may also cause a reaction.

7

What's a Reaction Like?

People with peanut allergies have to be careful! Eating peanuts can cause **hives**, breathing problems, and itchy eyes and throat. Some people might feel sick or throw up.

9

A very bad allergic reaction is called anaphylaxis (aa-nuh-fuh-LAK-suhs). It can include breathing problems, dizziness, and worse. Peanut allergies cause anaphylaxis more than any other food allergy.

Take the Test

If you've had an allergic reaction, you can be tested for a peanut allergy. In a skin **prick** test, a tiny amount of peanut is allowed under your skin. If a reaction occurs there, you've got a peanut allergy.

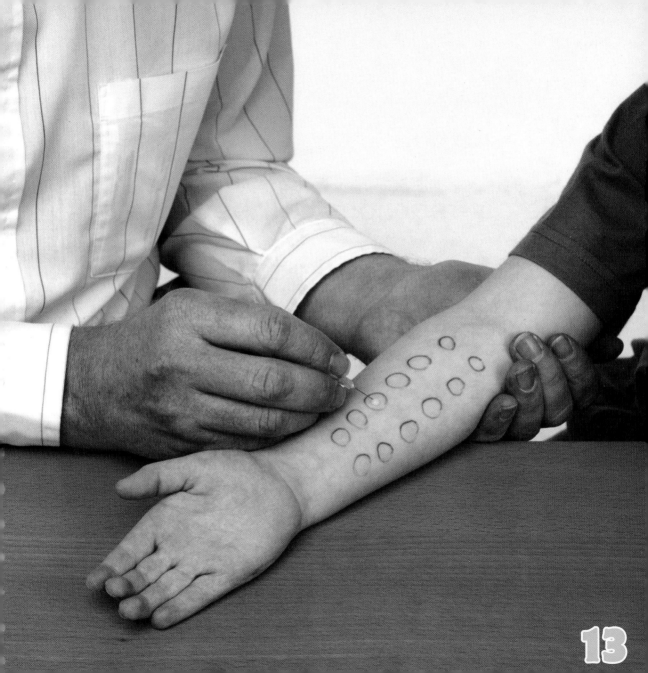

13

No Cure

Allergic reactions can be treated by a shot of a drug called epinephrine (eh-puh-NEH-fruhn). But right now, there's no way to **cure** peanut allergies. About 20 percent of children with peanut allergies outgrow them, though.

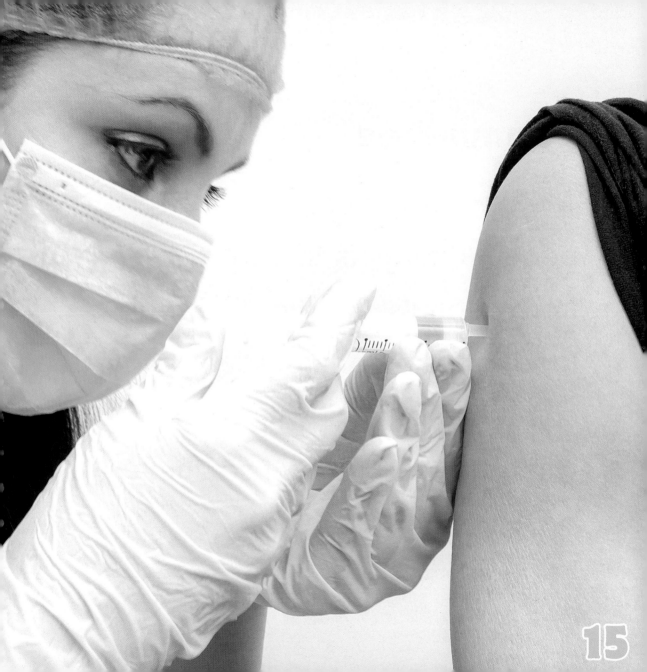

Peanut-Free

The best way to deal with a peanut allergy is to stay away from peanuts! You have to read food labels. Many products may come into contact with peanuts when they're made. If so, their package must say that.

...COLA...
...ARLEY FLAKE...
...OASTED WHEAT...
...MILK CHOCOLATE...
AND WHITE CHOCOLATE CO...

not suitable for

nut

allergy sufferers

V

VEGETARIAN

INGREDIENTS

Mixed Cereals (19%)

Raisins (16%)

...lgian Milk Chocolate

...Syrup

...Ch...

17

Those with peanut allergies can't eat peanut butter or peanuts. Peanuts can be found in many common food items. Cereals, cookies, ice cream, and bread are just some of the foods that could have peanuts in them.

Tree Nuts

Almonds, walnuts, pecans, and other nuts are tree nuts. Peanuts aren't tree nuts, but many people who are allergic to peanuts also have reactions to tree nuts. It's best for those who are allergic to stay away from them all.

21

GLOSSARY

allergy: a body's sensitivity to usually harmless things in the surroundings, such as dust, pollen, or foods

cure: to make healthy after an illness

hives: raised, itchy patches of skin that are redder or paler than the skin around them

prick: to cut slightly with a sharp point

protein: one of the building blocks of food

react: respond

BOOKS

Gordon, Sherri Mabry. *Are You at Risk for Food Allergies? Peanut Butter, Milk, and Other Deadly Threats.* Berkeley Heights, NJ: Enslow Publishers, Inc., 2014.

Mehra, Heather, and Kerry McManama. *Peanut-Free Tea for Three.* Newton, MA: Parent Perks, Inc., 2009.

WEBSITES

Just for Kids: Allergies and Asthma
www.aaaai.org/conditions-and-treatments/just-for-kids.aspx
Use the puzzles, games, and videos on this website to learn more about asthma and allergies.

Nut and Peanut Allergy
kidshealth.org/kid/stay_healthy/food/nut_allergy.html
Read more about peanut and nut allergies on the Kids Health website.

INDEX

24